THE LOST ART OF PIE MAKING

MADE EASY

by
Barbara Swell

Photo courtesy of the Library of Congress

ISBN 978-1883206420   Order No. NGB-838
Library of Congress Control Number: 2004100050
©2004 by Native Ground Books & Music, Inc.
Asheville, North Carolina

DARN GOOD PIE

What is it with pie and perfect? Surely that's something modern cookbook authors have dreamed up. Sure, you probably want your neurosurgeon to get things exactly right, but not so with your pie baking. Save perfection for special uppity occasion tart-baking, and maybe pie contests. It's the old fashioned, light brown, flaky, slightly lopsided pie with the bubbled-over fruit filling that warms our hearts. No, we're not going to make perfect pies, we're going to make darn good pies! Your house will smell as good as a silver haired, loving, sweet-scented old timey grandmother. When your family and friends see your homemade blueberry pie summer-breeze cooling on the windowsill, they'll claim you as their new best friend. Why, before you know it, you'll be whipping out those beauties in a flash saying, "I can't stop baking pies!"

Many of the recipes in this book come from historic sources. They are presented to you exactly as originally written in order to preserve the folklore of each recipe. Because our tastes have changed a bit over the years, any alterations I've made can be found either in parentheses or as an author's note.

And, by the way, just in case you think pie will make you fat, listen to this. I like to stay slim probably more than I like to eat, but this project has presented me with the ultimate challenge. After all, I've had to eat pie most every day for 6 months in order to be sure that all these pie recipes passed our rigid darn-good taste standards. One day, I'll write a book called, *The Pie Diet*, but for now, I've devised a pie work-off system. Let's say you want to eat a nice piece of apple pie with a lattice-topped crust. In order to neutralize those 400 or so calories, you can:

Rearrange the furniture	*1 hr. 15 min.*
Walk the dog	*1 hr. 45 min.*
Swing dance	*2 hr.*
Brush your teeth	*3 hr.*
Iron	*3 hr. 15 min.*
Kiss	*7 hr.*

Well, I'm the same size I was 100 pies ago. I'll leave the rest to your imagination! Enjoy!

CONTENTS

ADDITIONAL RECIPES & PIE MAKING TIPS

It's now 2014. Ten years and a thousand pies later, I'd like to share with you some additional pie making tips. Visit me at **www.logcabincooking.com** and go to the tutorial page.

THE LOST ART OF PIE

Time was when an American woman's worth was inextricably connected to her ability to turn out a dandy homemade pie with a flaky crust. Sure, men of yesterday frequently created attractive and tasty pies, but they were mostly doing a bit of artistic dabbling, for their worth was tied to being able to support the family and play a good game of golf with the boys.

Then along came the 1960s and 70s. Stampedes of liberated perky housewives traded in their aprons and rolling pins for psychedelic colored muumuus and jobs outside the home. And what did these women leave in their wake?

Just look at the wiggly red and green gelatin pies infused with bananas, strawberries, and artificial whipped topping squatting in store-bought pie crusts! These were bad times indeed, for lovers of down home old-timey pie.

By the 1980s, elaborate gourmet pies graced the covers of popular cooking and women's magazines. Now, women got up at 4 a.m., slid the Chocolate Mousse Raspberry Truffle Tart in the fridge before getting the family off to school, putting in a grueling day at the office, taking the kids to soccer practice, picking up the baby-sitter, and changing into the lovely-yet-casual black tunic top and stirrup pants. All fresh and ready to entertain!

Somewhere between gelatin pies and truffle tarts came a longing for the comfort foods and homey goodness of a simpler time. And that brings us to now. Pie is slow food in a too-fast world. Pie is a loving gesture. Good pie is simple and wholesome and real. You know what else pie is? Pie is sitting on the front porch glider having a lively conversation with family and friends, even though it's hot outside and there are a few mosquitos to swat. It's kids playing in the woods, crisp cotton sheets drying on the clothes line, crickets humming in the backyard, and time enough to play croquet. Pie is home.

THE PIE CONTEST

About a year ago, I became obsessed with pie. My family and several friends caught the pie fever as we took to the task of outdoing each other piewise. Well, it snowballed, and the piefest was born. Last July, with summer berries bursting on the vines, 75 contestants bedecked in pre-1970s attire, showed up at our door with some 42 homemade pies. The made-from-scratch gems were scattered throughout the house and yard, separated into 12 categories. Everyone was a judge, and the competition was fierce as we did our best to taste a bit of each and every one of the 42 pies.

The score cards were tallied, and retro prizes awarded in each pie category in addition to *best looking pie, best costume, most creative, best crust,* and the coveted *best in show pie.* You'll find several of the winning pie recipes as well as photos of the creators scattered throughout this book.

The second annual piefest promises to be even bigger and better as word is out now, and contestants are perfecting their pie baking skills and combing vintage clothing stores for just the right duds. In case you want to get pie fever going around where you live, I've included a few suggestions for hosting your own piefest on the following page.

Rowdy contestants whoop it up at the July 2003 Asheville piefest

THE PIE CONTEST

HOW TO HOST YOUR OWN PIE CONTEST

Invitations:
Send out 4 weeks in advance so contestants have a chance to practice pie baking and find their costumes. Old advertising cookbooklets contain fun graphics for your invitation.

Include and elaborate on "rules" like:
- Bring a pie that you bake (or a friend who bakes pie)
- No store bought crust or canned filling
- Come dressed in pre-1970 pie era attire

Set a time frame such as:
Arrive at 2:00, begin judging 2:30, prizes awarded at 4:00

Categories:
Contestants pick the categories, the more the better!
- Fruit
- Nut (pecan, peanut butter, walnut)
- Cream (filling cooked separate, added to a baked crust)
- Custard (filling cooked in the crust)
- Chiffon, mousse and whipped things some people call pie
- Chocolate
- Heirloom (old fashioned from a passed-down recipe)
- Cobbler, crisp, quick pie
- Savory meat or vegetable
- Youth (under 18, all the youth get a prize)
- 1st pie made

Photo by Richard Renfro

Possible retro prizes:
Shop on-line auctions, antique stores, estate auctions and yard sales. Most of these can be found for $1-$10:

Wood handle pastry cutters, pie jagger/crimpers, pie wedges, well worn rolling pins, vintage glass pie plates and tins, retro kitchenware, gently used crocheted pot holders, aprons, aprons, and aprons.

THE PIE CONTEST

It seems like yesterday that pie was the favorite invited guest of just about every American celebration. We're not just talking about holiday meals, either. Up through the 1950s, pie eating contests were frequently an exciting part of community festivities. Pie auctions not only raised money for neighborhood schools and churches, they provided the young folks with some much needed wholesome courting opportunities. And the ultimate venue for showcasing those special pie baking talents? The county and state fair. Why not invite pie to your next gathering and see if it doesn't bring out a little competitive spirit in you.

Photo by Russell Lee Courtesy Library of Congress

Pie eating contest at the 1939 4-H club fair in Cimarron, Kansas

---

Pie and Marriage
Kentucky Superstitions

- *If you eat the point of a piece of pie first, you will be an old maid.*
- *If a piece of pie is placed before you at the table with the crust toward you, you will be an old maid.*
- *If you take the last piece of pie on a plate, you will get a handsome husband or a beautiful wife.*

THE PIE AUNTS

If you don't have a real aunt or other friend who can show you in person how to make a dandy pie, don't worry. The perky 1930s and 40s Aunt Jenny and Aunt Chick can help. Their entertaining cookbooklets are easy to find on-line, and these ladies are a hoot. Let me introduce you to each:

AUNT CHICK

Aunt Chick

While Nettie McBirney was editing the 1930s food column in the Tulsa Daily World called "The Kitchen Log," she discovered something shocking. Yes, she discovered that nine out of ten women were afraid of pies. That's right. Afraid of pies! So under the pen name of Aunt Chick, this clever inventor of the *Crispy Crust Pie Pan* and the *Non-Stick Pastry Canvas* wrote a little cookbook to "eliminate the scare" of pies from women forever. Indeed, Aunt Chick has cured me.

"Aunt Chick's Pies" gives detailed instructions with plenty of photos and includes the recipes for 150 old-timey pies in just 39 pages! Not only that, there are pie tips at the bottom of each page. You can read more about her as well as order some of her coveted, non stick cookie cutters at *www.grammascutters.com*. You'll find Aunt Chick's pie recipes and tips scattered throughout this book.

"I make you pay for this book because you have no respect for, or faith in, a free one."
-Aunt Chick

THE PIE AUNTS

AUNT JENNY

The hit radio program *Aunt Jenny's Real Life Stories* debuted on CBS in 1937. Aunt Jenny, played by Edith Spencer, narrated short stories about the everyday adventures of residents of small town Littleton. Following the show, Aunt Jenny would enthusiastically share a recipe featuring the show's sponsor, Spry shortening. Edith Spencer also appeared in Spry's very entertaining recipe cookbooklets until some time in the 1940s, when she left the show. The absent Edith appeared as a cartoon in the 1949 recipe book, and then in 1953, the new Aunt Jenny was altogether tame. The still inexpensive cookbooks are easy to find and they are a scream.

The many faces of Aunt Jenny

Late 1930s   1949   1953

PIE CRUST

A unt Chick was right when she said, *"Don't be scared. It is just pie crust."* So what! That said, here are some helpful techniques to get you on your way to a darn good pie crust. Just remember to have fun, practice, and find a mentor.

PIE PANS:

Clear glass is the best, you can see how the bottom crust is doing, and it won't be soggy. I prefer vintage Pyrex or Fire King. They're shallow and come in a multitude of sizes. And, because busy people don't bake pies any more, you can pick them up at yard sales for next to nothing.

INGREDIENTS

FLOUR:

You have to understand flour to achieve your ultimate goal ... a crust that's both tender and flaky. For tender crust, gluten (the protein in flour) is the enemy. If you're making bread, then it's your buddy. So don't use bread flour. I prefer unbleached flour for both color and taste. King Arthur makes a nice unbleached all purpose flour that works well for crust, and it's nationally available. Pastry flour will yield a tender crust, but one that is difficult to roll out. Some prefer to use half pastry and half all purpose flour. Whole wheat pastry flour makes a good crust for a vegetable or meat pie, but regular whole wheat flour produces a tough and earthy tasting crust. Here in Asheville, we now have fantastic locally-grown and milled organic low protein flours available to home bakers. If you come across a regional artisan flour, grab it!

PIE CRUST

Butter

Lard

Crisco

FATS:

Shortening: Crisco made its way into American pantries in 1911. At a time when butter was often rancid, and lard imparted an undesirable pork flavor to food; solid shortenings made from vegetable oil touted to be "pure, white, and digestible" were a welcome relief to pie bakers. Fats like Crisco, Spry, and Jewell contained no water (pie crust's greatest enemy), and stayed fresh unrefrigerated for long periods of time. In addition to Crisco, there are a number of "natural" and organic trans-fat free solid shortenings available to pie bakers. Coconut oil is also an option for vegan crusts. These fats are easier to work with when frozen.

Lard: My father, Leon Swell, insists that lard is the only suitable shortening for pie crust. This from a man who spent 35 years of his life as a biochemist researching cholesterol. Leaf lard from the kidney area of the hog is the best, but it's hard to find. You surely will get a tender crust, but be sure to let your guests know. A vegetarian will be able to taste the lard and you don't want them to ruin your pie-eating experience when they freak out after eating a bite of your beautiful pie.

Oil: Makes a tender crust, especially good for Pennsylvania Dutch style pies. See page 53 for recipe.

Unsalted Butter: That's the one for me. The flavor and crispiness imparted by butter is just fabulous in any kind of pie. Be sure to use unsalted, and buy the best quality you can find. Plugra is a European style butter that performs consistently well, as do most of the organic varieties. Some brands contain more water than others, you'll have to experiment to see which works best for you. Don't substitute margarine or spreads, they contain too much water, and will make your crust tough.

Pie Crust Recipes

Barb's Butter Crust

2½ cups all purpose flour (350 g. or 12.3 oz.)
1 tsp. fine salt
Pinch baking powder
1 cup (8 oz./2 sticks) COLD unsalted butter
½ cup (4 oz.) ice water
2 tsp. lemon juice

This makes two pie crusts. Mix the dry ingredients. Cut butter into ½-inch cubes and divide into two piles. Put one pile in the freezer. Cut the remaining half of the butter into the flour with a pastry cutter or TIPS of your fingers, until the mixture resembles coarse crumbs (for tenderness.) Now fetch the rest of the butter from the freezer and mix it into the flour until it's the size of small peas (for flakiness.) Be sure to work fast! You want your fat to stay cold. If it melts, your crust won't be flaky. Now for the tricky part. Add the lemon juice into your ice water, and sprinkle the water into your flour, one tablespoon at a time, tossing the mixture with a fork. You want the dough to stick together when squeezed, but it will be a bit dry. Too much water makes a tough crust. Too little and your dough won't hold together. Divide into two balls, flattening them a bit. Wrap each in plastic wrap and refrigerate for a minimum of 30 minutes or, even better, overnight. Don't skip this step!

When you're ready to roll, put dough onto a barely floured board and let it sit out about 15 minutes until workable, but cold. Roll it out as thin as you can from the inside out, giving dough a quarter turn with each couple rolls. You want it to be 1½ inch bigger than the top of your pie pan all the way around. (Lay your pie pan on your dough upside down and trim the jagged edges of your dough with a knife) When you place your crust in your pan, be sure not to stretch it to fit. The dough "remembers" it's original shape and will shrink itself back down when baked.

Author's note: The acid in lemon juice prevents gluten from developing, as does covering each speck of flour with a little fat when the first half of the butter is added. The 1930s pie Aunts taught me that baking powder gives the crust a little lift, making it more flaky.

PIE CRUST RECIPES

PSSST ... A FLAKY CRUST SECRET

Okay, this advanced crust technique will change your life and make your butter crust behave like a puff paste. I call it **The Schmear.** French bakers call it fraisage. Instead of pressing your dough into two patties, freeze the moist crumbs a minute to get them good and cold while you tidy up your kitchen. Toss the chilled dough crumbs onto your board, dividing them into two piles. Using the heel of your hand, quickly smear the crumbs across an unfloured board or counter, about 4 inches or so, enough to flatten the butter. Stack up the smears into two piles and then form into patties. Refrigerate overnight. For a visual schmear tutorial, visit *www.logcabincooking.com.*

SHORTENING CRUST

For an all-shortening crust, see page 67, Mom Brookes' flaky crust. Using half shortening (or lard) and half butter also makes a decent crust that holds its decorative crimp well when baked. Follow the butter crust recipe and substitute ½ cup frozen shortening or lard chunks for the first half of the butter, working it into the flour until the mixture is crumbly.

Making a decorative
fluted edge

Score edges with
fork.

To seal in juices, fold top crust over bottom and crimp with fork

PIE HINTS

A Word About Bubbled-Over Pie Filling ...

I used to think this was a bad thing, a sign of an inexperienced pie baker. After extensive research in the form of serving bubbled-over pie to a plethora of tasters, here's my current position: People get real excited about a bubbled-over pie. They see that purple juice sitting on top of the flaky pie crust and they're ready to dig in. It doesn't matter if it's a lattice or a solid top pie crust, people have the same reaction. Pie lust. Pie juice spilled on the oven is another matter. It will quickly burn and smoke your pie as well as your house. So after the pie begins to bubble on the edges, place a couple pieces of foil on your oven floor to catch the drips.

You Really Need ...

Photo by Richard Renfro

Aluminum foil: Invaluable for protecting crust from burning and your oven from pie juice drippings. Remember the shiny side reflects heat, so keep the dull side facing heating elements.

Parchment paper: You can reuse it many times. Use it to roll your crust out on and for blind baking. You can also use a pastry cloth if you like.

Pastry cutter: Such a wonderful tool for cutting in your fat. Go for retro and find a vintage cutter with a painted wooden handle.

Pie crimper or jagger: So much fun! You have to have one. My favorite is a 19th century brass beauty that I bought for ten bucks at an on-line auction.

Rita Erbsen and Sara Webb decked out in their retro pie baking attire

A vintage apron: Our favorite part of pie-baking. These will get you in the mood. They're inexpensive, and like antique pie plates, people just don't know the true value of the hand sewn feedsack 1940s apron adorned with rick rack!

Pie Hints

Blind Baking

This is just a pre-baked bottom pie crust. Place the pastry in your pan, turn edges under and flute. Chill at least 30 minutes. Cut a piece of parchment paper into a big circle and put it on your crust. Fill crust up to the edges with either beans, rice, or ceramic pie weights (or place another pie plate the same size on top of the parchment paper). Bake in bottom third of a 425° oven for 15 minutes. Remove paper and weights, prick with a fork all over and bake for about 7 more minutes until lightly browned. Or, you can do as Aunt Chick suggested in 1949:

"I find that when I bake it at 350° for 12 minutes, then raise to 425°, I have a more well behaved crust."

Use a Lattice Crust on Fruit Pies When ...

- You want to show off the fruit filling inside. Pretty much, you want to always show off a red pie.
- You want to be sure the center is fully bubbling.
- You want a fancy pie.

Use One Crust ...

For custard, cream, nut pies, and tarts. Tarts are the old-fashioned American pie's attractive, uppity cousin. While they are delicious, we're sticking with down-home pie in this book.

Bettina makes an apple pie for her husband, Bob. Read more about how she keeps her new husband happy on page 40.

MERINGUE

***M**eringue is making me crazy. Everybody who makes a beautiful and tasty meringue has their own foolproof method, none of which works for me. It's probably because I don't like fluffy food and I try to convince the meringue to be something it's not supposed to be. But, because I have confidence in YOUR abilities, I*  *will share with you all my hard-earned knowledge about my foamy nemesis.*

TRADITIONAL MERINGUE
Galax Cook Book, Famous Recipes from Old Virginia, 1976

> 3 egg whites (room temperature)
> ¼ tsp. cream of tartar (stabilizes the whites)
> 6 Tbs. granulated sugar

"When ready to make meringue, start heating oven at 350°. Place whites in a medium bowl, add cream of tartar. Start beating until frothy throughout. Start adding sugar a little at a time to frothy whites, beating well after each addition. Added this early, sugar dissolves better. Continue beating until stiff peaks are formed. The peaks should be so stiff they don't curl over. Spread on pie, touching inner edge of crust all around (very important). Bake 15 minutes. Place on lowest rack if browning too quickly."

HOW MERINGUE CAN MAKE YOU CRAZY, TOO

To Keep Crust Crisp
Pour cooled filling into crust, then top with meringue.

To Keep Cream Filling From Weeping
Pour hot filling into crust, then top with meringue.

To Keep From Being Poisoned By Salmonella Bacteria
Add hot filling to hot crust, which will become soggy. Then top with meringue that you bake until it's rubbery.

MERINGUE

COOKED MERINGUE

The chances of contracting Salmonellosis from raw eggs is remote, but if you've ever had it, as I have, you won't go near a raw egg ever again. Here's the safest method of being sure your whites are cooked enough (to 160° F) to remove any risk.

In a (non aluminium)* double boiler, stir together:

> **3 egg whites**
> **6 heaping Tbs. sugar**
> **¼ tsp. cream of tartar**
> **3 tsp. water**

Cook over simmering water while beating with an electric mixer on low speed until mixture reaches 160°. Remove from heat and pour into medium bowl. Beat on high until stiff peaks are formed.

*If you use an aluminum pan, your meringue will be gray!

MERINGUE MISERIES

Beads form on top of meringue.
Your sugar did not dissolve completely. Add it earlier, right when the whites start to foam, and add it gradually.

The meringue is an island in the middle of your pie.
You didn't anchor the edges of the meringue well enough to the pie crust before baking.

Meringue is the consistency of foam packing peanuts.
You beat it too long, or overbaked it at too high a temperature.

MEN LOVE PIE

Men LOVE pie! After exhaustive research on the topic, I'll tell you how I know. Whenever I mention pie to a man, there's a 99% chance he will say: "Oh, I just love pie." I must say that I always ask, "Why?" Invariably, the answer is, "Well, I just do." You see, women usually say they like pie, then they go on (and on) about what kinds of pie they like or don't like, and it usually turns out that they really prefer chocolate cake. In case you don't believe that men love pie, here's some carefully selected historical evidence that proves my point:

Exhibit 1:
Vintage cookbook quotes:
"Dear to the heart of man and boys is the meringue pie."
-Good Pies Easy to Make, 1920s
"Pies are the American man's favorite."
-Tested Recipes with Jewel Shortening, 1930s
"Pie is man's most appealing dish."
-How Mama Could Cook, 1946
"Nearly every man loves pie!"
-12 Pies Husbands like best, 1952

Exhibit 2:
The most compelling piece of evidence:
Get a copy of the March, 1940 issue of *Farm Journal and Farmer's Wife* magazine. There's a whole section dedicated to the demise of he-man meals. The editor has this to say about what 1940s men were missing when their wives started making more sensible, lower calorie meals for their farm husbands:

> *"And Pie! How men hunger for good flaky, crusted, pie. None of these chiffony things, mind you, but first class apple, pumpkin, custard, or cherry pie."*

The 12 pies husbands like best? Chocolate Cream, Blueberry, Pumpkin, Apple, Banana Cream, Butterscotch, Lemon Meringue, Cherry, Coconut Custard, Peach, Apple Crumb, and Steak.

MEN LOVE PIE

THE SECRET OF WHY MEN LOVE PIE

I didn't spend 15 years as a psychotherapist for nothing. Since men act like they don't even know why they LOVE pie, I have had to come up with my own psychological theory based on countless hours of time spent around men, including my own pie-lovin' husband, Wayne. Here are the official reasons why men love pie:

- *When men eat pie, they think somebody is taking care of them.*
- *Pie is home, no matter where you are. Men love home.*
- *Men want their bellies to be full, and pie is filling.*
- *Pie has intrigue. Pie is adventure, mystery, romance, and love.*
- *Pie is what it is ... uncomplicated, honest and good.*

HOW A LADY CAN BEST USE THIS SECRET INFORMATION

Why, just this fall, my daughter, Annie, set one of her gorgeous apple pies on the windowsill of her college dorm room to cool. A young male classmate walked by outside, saw it, and called up to her, "What do I have to do to get that pie?" As luck would have it, he was training to be a masseuse. The two hour massage she traded for the pretty pie was just the antidote she needed for her overly ambitious course-load. And the young man ... he finished off that apple pie in one evening!

Annie Erbsen with her peach raspberry-blueberry pie

FRUIT PIES

~~~~~~~~~~~~~~~~~~~~~~~

THE PERFECT FRUIT PIE

Pie Marches On, Monroe Strause, *1951*

"Visualize if you can, what I term a perfect fruit pie. It must have a good rich crust, be thoroughly baked, and when it is cut, the firm fruit should roll gently from beneath its crust; and its filling or juices must be transformed into syrup, not into a thick cornstarch mass."   -Monroe Boston Strause, "The Pie King"

Good thing we're not going for perfect, because if you made pies the way The Pie King suggested, that's all you'd have time to do. He was, however, in the restaurant pie business, and back in the 1930s-50s, folks were loyal to a restaurant whose pies were excellent. Hey, remember when restaurants served regular sized meal portions and you had room for dessert? Though Monroe Strause's techniques are tedious and foolproof, his book is entertaining. I guarantee you WILL win the pie contest if you follow his instructions. I've included his unique rhubarb pie recipe on page 23, since that's a difficult pie to get right.

Thickeners for Fruit Pies

Flour is an old-timey thickener. I like a little in apple and peach pies. Four tablespoons of flour has the same thickening ability as three tablespoons of either cornstarch or tapioca.

Cornstarch becomes clear and thick once it has boiled a few minutes. It's the most popular thickener for pies. You really need to be sure the pie has boiled clear through to the middle for several minutes in order for this thickener to do its job.

Tapioca flour (starch) is the most aggressive thickener. Use it for blueberry, blackberry, and rhubarb pies to ensure a good set. I prefer it to cornstarch because you won't get the dreaded raw starch taste if it hasn't boiled enough in the center of your pie. As long as most of your pie is good and bubbly, you're good to go. Substitute equal amounts of tapioca flour for cornstarch in most recipes.

Hint: Add a handful of dried fruit to your pies to insure set and boost your flavor. (See July Berry Pie, page 27)

FRUIT PIES

Sweetness Warning

I have to warn you that, even though I'm technically a Southerner, I'm not a fan of sweet, sweet fruit pies. Sugar covers up the fresh flavor of summer fruit, and that's criminal, if you ask me. There's sugar-preference wiggle room in most of these recipes, look for options in parentheses. Fruit jams can also sweeten your pies and intensify the flavors.

SIMPLE SUMMER FRUIT PIE

Use fresh fruit in season, locally grown is best. For a 9-inch shallow pie pan, fill with about 6 cups of fruit, add 3 Tbs. cornstarch or tapioca and ½ cup sugar. If you love sweet pies, increase to ¾ cup. Always adjust your sugar to the sweet or tartness of your fruit. For a beautiful top crust, brush the pastry (but not the edges) with half and half or cream and sprinkle with a little sugar before baking.

BAKING

No two experts can agree on time and temperature for baking fruit pies. That tells me it doesn't really matter. You'll get darn good results if you relax, practice, and:

1. Start the pie off in a hot 425° oven for 12 minutes, then turn the heat to 375° for fruit, or 350° if the pie contains eggs, and bake for another 30-45 minutes or so, until done.
2. Bake the pie on the lowest shelf of your gas oven or lowest third, electric oven, to yield a crispy, never soggy, bottom crust.
3. Allow the filling to totally bubble for a few minutes in the innermost part of the pie to insure a filling that "sets."
4. Cover the edges of your crust with a bit of foil if it's browning too quickly.
5. Hang around the kitchen and keep an eye on your delicious piece of art so it's doesn't get overbaked.

FRUIT PIES

FRESH STRAWBERRY PIE

Spring's here, and it's strawberry picking time! Locally grown berries are an absolute must for this refreshing pie. The sweet small to medium sized red ripe berries work best.

> **3 pints fresh strawberries**
> **½ to ¾ cup sugar**
> **3 Tbs. cornstarch dissolved in ¼ cup water**
> **2 Tbs. lemon juice or black raspberry liquor**
> **A baked and cooled 9-inch pie crust**

Slice the caps off washed and dried strawberries. Place two cups of berries in a saucepan and crush with a potato masher. Add sugar (more or less to your taste) and cornstarch dissolved in water. Bring slowly to a boil, stirring constantly. Simmer on low heat until thickened and clear, about 5 more minutes. Remove from stove, stir in lemon juice, and allow it to cool until it's just a bit warm. At this point, you can place the strawberries in a baked crust, pointed side up and pour glaze over, or you can stir in halved berries, then pour into your crust. Chill at least 3 hours until glaze sets up. Serve with freshly whipped cream.

Chocolate Strawberry Pie: Heat 4 Tbs. heavy cream to simmer and pour over 3 oz. chopped bittersweet chocolate. When chocolate melts, stir well and brush onto pre-baked crust. Chill briefly before adding strawberries.

The "Pie King," Monroe Strause shows off his fragrant pie.

Fruit Pies

The Pie King's Fresh Rhubarb Pie
Pie Marches On, 1951

"One of the greatest evils in fresh rhubarb is the amount of thickening necessary to keep the pie from being sloppy," says Monroe Strause, author of "Pie Marches On." So, in order to avoid having a runny or gluey pie, clear your calendar for the day, get the kids out of the kitchen, and do the following:

Use early season tender rhubarb. Red stalks make a pretty pie. Green tastes fine, but your pie will look like it's made with celery. Wash and chop fresh rhubarb into ¾ inch long pieces. You should have about 4 cups. Mix the rhubarb with one cup sugar and let it sit in a colander (at room temperature) with a bowl underneath for 2-3 hours. No more than three! Pile the drained rhubarb in an unbaked crust. Cover with a solid top crust, being sure there are absolutely no tears or holes anywhere. Now, brush edges with water and crimp well to seal. Poke one hole the size of your index finger in the very top of the pie (the large end of a pastry tip works well.)

This technique won't work if there are any tears or thin spots in your top crust. Wash the top with melted butter, and let it dry before baking. Timing is crucial for this next part. Bake at 450° for 35 minutes. Meanwhile, pour your sugar/rhubarb syrup into a saucepan, add 1/6 cup corn syrup, and cook to 242°. Don't stir once it starts to boil. When your pie has been out of the oven 5 to 10 minutes, carefully pour one cup of the hot syrup into the pie via that little hole in the top crust.

Author's note: I don't have to tell you how dangerous it is to handle hot syrup like this. Use a glass liquid measuring cup to pour the syrup into that little hole, but please be careful. Don't even make this if you have kids in your kitchen.

FRUIT PIES

STRAWBERRY RHUBARB PIE

3 cups fresh rhubarb cut into ½-inch slices
2 cups sliced fresh strawberries
½-¾ cup sugar, according to your preference
3 Tbs. tapioca flour (or corn starch)
1 tsp. lemon or orange zest
Two 9-inch unbaked pie crusts

Mix sugar and tapioca flour and toss with rhubarb. Let mixture sit about 15 minutes. Stir in strawberries and lemon zest. Pour into an unbaked shell. Top with lattice crust. Bake at 425° 10 minutes and reduce heat to 375° and continue to bake about 30 minutes until filling bubbles all the way through.

Courtesy of the Library of Congress

"Salvation Army girls with steel helmets and gas masks make pies for free each day for the solders, 26th Division, Ansonville, France" May 9, 1918

FRUIT PIES

DOUBLE SOUR CHERRY AMARETTO PIE

If you aren't able to get your hands on fresh sour cherries, canned cherries will do. Drain the juice, then use it to flavor your iced tea. You can use sweet cherries as well, just adjust the sugar.

> 4 cups Montmorency (sour) cherries
> ¾ cup sugar (½ cup for a tart pie)
> 2 Tbs. cornstarch or tapioca flour
> ½ cup dried sour cherries
> 3 Tbs. Amaretto

Soak dried cherries in warm Amaretto at least 15 minutes. Toss pitted fresh cherries with sugar and cornstarch, then add dried cherry mixture. Place in a 9-inch unbaked crust, and top with lattice strips. Bake in the bottom third of a 425° oven 10 minutes then reduce heat to 375° and bake another 30 minutes or so until filling bubbles.

Author's note: Rhubarb sour cherry pie is fabulous as well. Just replace the fresh cherries with an equal amount of rhubarb.

How to Pit Cherries, 1857
The Great Western Cook Book or Table Receipts

"Cut a quill as if you were going to make a pen, only, instead of its being sharp, it must be round at the end; hold the cherry in your left hand, and with the other, push the quill into it by the side of the stalk, as far as the top of the stone; then take hold of the stalk, and with the aid of the quill, pull the stone out of the stalk, without breaking the fruit in pieces."

FRUIT PIES

AUNT EVA'S FRESH BLUEBERRY PIE

What a dilemma. You have a bucket of fresh-picked blueberries and you want to make a pie. But the berries are so sweet and delicious, you can't bear to bake them. Thanks to my friend, Pam Budd, and her baking wizard Great Aunt Eva, we have the perfect solution ... a pie that blends the great flavors of fresh and cooked blueberries all in one!

¾ cup sugar	½ cup water
2 Tbs. cornstarch	4 cups blueberries
Pinch salt	1½ Tbs. lemon juice
2 Tbs. butter	Fresh whipped cream

Combine sugar (adjust to your taste and the sweetness of your berries), cornstarch, and salt in a saucepan. Blend with the water and 2 cups of the blueberries. Bring to a boil while mashing the berries. Cook until thickened and translucent, then stir in the lemon juice and butter. When mixture is cool, stir in remaining 2 cups fresh berries. Line a baked pie shell with a small amount of whipped cream. Spread the filling on this, and top with more whipped cream. Serve immediately.

Photo by Richard Renfro

Pam says: If you don't plan to eat the pie right away, omit the whipped cream from under and on top of the pie. Frost pie with whipped cream just before serving.

Pam Budd and her Aunt Eva's Fresh Blueberry Pie

FRUIT PIES

FOOD AND HEALTH

DOUBLE CRUST JULY FRESH BERRY PIE

2 cups blueberries	½ cup dried blueberries (opt.)
2 cups raspberries	½ (up to ¾ cup) sugar
2 cups wild blackberries	3 Tbs. tapioca flour

Combine sugar, tapioca and fruit. Fill unbaked bottom crust with mixture and top with a solid, vented crust. Seal edges and crimp. This is such a special pie, why don't you go ahead and decorate the top with a sprig of blueberries made from dough scraps? Brush the top with cream or milk and strew with sugar. Bake in a 425° oven for 15 minutes. Reduce heat to 375° and bake another 35-40 minutes until filling bubbles. You may need to protect the crust with foil if it's browning too quickly. And put foil on your oven floor; this pie will drip. Remember pie bubblage is beautiful!

FRUIT PIES

RASPBERRIES IN AMBUSH
The Ladies Home Journal , June 1887

This is the suggested dessert to serve with your 1887 Sunday cottage dinner that also includes brown fricasseed chicken, boiled potatoes, and string beans. Works for me!

"Make a nice pastry and line a pie plate with it. Bake in a quick oven and while warm, spread thickly with red raspberries and heap on these a meringue made of the whites of four eggs beaten stiff with half a cupful of powdered sugar. Mix a handful of raspberries through the meringue. Brown very lightly and eat soon afterwards, when it is cool."

SO MANY LADIES ASKED ME HOW I MAKE TENDER, FLAKY, DIGESTIBLE PIE CRUST THAT I'M SHOWIN' HOW HERE. IT'S EASY AS ROLLIN' OFF A LOG IF YOU USE SPRY AN' DO IT THIS WAY...

FRESH RASPBERRY PIE

This pie is best with the big, fat locally grown raspberries you pick yourself. In a pinch, you can make it with frozen berries.

Pre-bake and cool a 9-inch pie shell. In a saucepan, combine:

1 cup crushed raspberries
½ cup water

Cook a few minutes and strain to remove seeds. Dissolve 2 Tbs. cornstarch in ¼ cup cold water and add to the strained berries along with ½ cup sugar, more or less, depending on how sweet you like your pie. Cook on medium heat, stirring continuously until thickened and clear. Add a tablespoon of fresh lemon juice and let mixture cool off a tad. Line the bottom of the baked crust with 3 or 4 cups fresh raspberries. Pour the warm sauce over the berries, and refrigerate. Serve chilled with whipped cream and garnish with a little lemon zest.

FRUIT PIES

GREEN APPLE & LEMON SLICE PIE
Ladies' Home Journal, August, 1887

Now, here's a dandy pie to make with your not-quite-ripe fall apples. Popular in women's magazines in the 1880s, this unusual and delicious pie packs a punch between the tart apples and the lemon slices. If you don't have an apple tree, you can substitute Granny Smith or other tart apples.

"Peel and slice juicy, tart apples and fill a shell of paste with them. Strew thickly with sugar and scatter thin slices of lemon here and there. Cover with a top crust. Eat warm, with sweet cream and plenty of sugar."

Author's note: Use apples that are almost ripe and adjust your sugar according to your taste.

> **6 cups pared, sliced, just under-ripe or tart apples**
> **½ cup brown sugar and ¼ cup white sugar**
> **2 Tbs. flour**
> **½ lemon, seeds removed, sliced paper thin**
> **A dab of butter**

Toss together all ingredients, pile into an unbaked shell, dot with butter. Cover with a top crust (not lattice), vent, and crimp. Bake in a 425° oven 15 minutes, then reduce heat to 375° and bake another 45 minutes or so , until filling bubbles and crust is brown.

1918 World War I poster

Fruit Pies

Nelle's Concord Grape Pie
Food Fit For a King, Salem W.Va. 1920s

This extroverted pie will jump up and scream "YEE-HAA" right in your face. Make it with your local slip-skin blue or red grapes for a flavor-bursting, tantalizing purple pie. Two crusts are needed to temper the intense flavor. If you have them, use miniature cookie cutters to cut out a few shapes in the top crust so you can see when the gorgeous filling is done. Traditional recipes call for one cup of sugar, but if you use sweet Concords, half that amount will be plenty.

> 1½ lb. Concord grapes (4 cups with stems removed)
> ½ cup sugar (or more depending on the grapes)
> 3 Tbs. tapioca or cornstarch
> Pinch salt
> 1 Tbs. butter

Separate pulp from skins. You'll want to end up with about one firmly packed cup of skins. Simmer the pulp in a covered saucepan on low about 5-10 minutes until the mixture is liquid. Strain the seeds. You should end up with about 1¼ cup pulp. You can add a little water if needed to make up the difference. Combine the tapioca starch, sugar, pulp, and the reserved skins, and pour into a 9-inch pie plate. Dot top with butter and cover with a solid, well-vented crust. Crimp with a fork. Bake in a preheated 425° oven for 15 minutes. Reduce heat to 375° and bake another 30 or so minutes until filling bubbles all the way through. If you have lots of grapes, freeze the skins and strained pulp together in amounts needed for each pie.

Fruit Pies

Dutch Oven Apple & Boozy Cherry Pie

Won't your friends and family be impressed when you whip out this delicious fireplace pie during your next winter blackout! You don't even have to wait for the power to go off, because it's easy to make for camping trips or backyard barbecues. Just be sure it's dark outside when you pull the pie from the fire because this is rustic pie baking at it's best. Really, a few ashes and burnt spots will only add to the homey hearth-baked experience.

Put a metal trivet (or three canning jar rings) in the bottom of a 12-inch, footed dutch oven. Assemble your pie in a 9-inch pie plate, and place it inside the preheated cast iron oven. Just stick it next to the fire to get it good and hot. Put a small shovel-full of coals underneath the pot and on top of the lid, and check the pie after about 45 minutes. Replace some of the coals as needed, and keep the pan away from the fire itself (so the sides don't burn.) You can make any pie this way, but here's one that always brings cheers when I make it for hearth-cooking demonstrations.

1 large plastic zip bag
5 cups firm cooking apples, sliced
2 Tbs. flour
½ cup brown sugar
A handful of dried cherries soaked in
3 Tbs. liqueur such as Calvados apple
brandy, Cointreau, rum or brandy

Roll out a top and bottom crust, and place between pieces of waxed paper. Keep chilled in your cooler. Line bottom of a 9-inch pie plate with crust. Peel and slice your apples and put them in a large zip bag. Mix the flour with the sugar, and toss to coat the apples. Stir in the boozy cherries. Top pie with a lattice crust (so you can see what's going on with the filling) and crimp rustically. Bake in dutch oven as instructed above.

FRUIT PIES

THE FAIR

Fueled by the success of our piefest in July, I decided I had to go for the ultimate prize in pie baking. The "Judge's Choice" pie ribbon at the Western North Carolina Mountain State Fair would be mine. After all, how could I write a pie cookbook if I couldn't bake such a worthy pie myself? The fair was just a few weeks away in September, and so I started on my pie rampage. Apples and red raspberries would be in season; that had to be a winning combination. After lots of practice and research, the day of judgement arrived. Armed with just the right old timey local pie apples, and fresh raspberries I picked myself, the apple-raspberry pie was born. It was a beauty. I also made an oatmeal coconut pie for old-time's sake and sent them on their way to the fairgrounds to be judged.

Three days I had to wait to see what fate had befallen my pies. As I entered the cavernous metal building, passed the 800-pound pumpkin, and 72-pound beet, I searched for the sea of pie entries among the long shelves of baked goods. There they were, all six of them in a refrigerated case. I had entered one third of the pies! The oatmeal pie was bedecked with blue, and what little was left of the apple pie was covered with two ribbons, including JUDGE'S CHOICE PIE!!! Feeling proud yet disappointed at the dearth of competition, a volunteer came around the corner and said, "the judges sure loved your pie. They almost ate it all up."

Next year, I bet they'll have more pie entries at the fair, because our pie baking community of folks will get in on the fun. I must tell you though, this pie is good. I bet if you enter it in your State or County Fair, you'll win a blue ribbon, too.

FRUIT PIES

BARB'S BLUE RIBBON APPLE-RASPBERRY PIE

Filling:

> 7 apples peeled and sliced ¼ inch thick (I used Cortland,
> Rome, and Green Pippin)
> 1 Tbs. butter
> ¼ cup sugar
> 1 Tbs. orange marmalade

Melt butter in a frying pan, cook apples and ¼ cup sugar, covered, 4 minutes. Remove apples, and reduce liquid to about 2 tablespoons. Add reduced liquid back to apples, along with the marmalade, and let mixture cool.

Then toss together in a separate bowl:

> 1 cup fresh raspberries
> ¼ cup sugar
> 2 Tbs. flour
> 3 Tbs. raspberry liqueur or Calvados (apple brandy)

Topping:

Blend:

> 6 Tbs. flour
> ¼ cup brown sugar
> 3 Tbs. chilled butter
> Handful chopped walnuts

SWELL APPLE PIE! SUCH TENDER FLAKY CRUST!

Layer half the apples on a chilled unbaked pie shell. Spread raspberry mixture on top of apples. Add remaining apples, then spread with topping mixture. For the top crust, cut 10 strips of dough about ½ inch wide with a pastry wheel or knife. Lay the first 5 strips across pie filling, then weave the remaining strips crossways. Fold dough from edges of lower pie crust over ends of strips and then crimp decoratively. Brush crust strips with a bit of cream, then sprinkle with a little cinnamon sugar and bake at 375° for about 1 hour and 15 minutes until filling bubbles.

LEMON PIES

If you look at mid-19th-century American cookbooks or hand-written cooking manuscripts, this is the pie that appears most often. Of course, western pioneers weren't making lemon pies, they rarely saw a lemon until the late 1860s when the railroad crossed the country. Vinegar pies were a popular substitute.

The lemon meringue pies of today haven't changed much since the 1850s, but we seldom see recipes anymore for a baked two crust lemon pie or lemon sponge pie. Try them all, especially if you have a man around because:

"Dear to the heart of man and boy is the Meringue Pie. Go into any restaurant, lunch room or cafeteria and see how quickly a flaky Lemon Meringue pie with creamy yellow filling, topped by a fluffy golden meringue, light as a summer breeze will disappear."

-Good Pies, Easy to Make, 1920s

MOM'S LEMON MERINGUE PIE

There's not a soul on earth that can out-lemon-meringue-pie my mother, Nancy Smith Swell. After baking, oh, maybe 500 of them, she was finally recognized as reigning lemon meringue pie champion at our 2003 summer pie contest. Long time overdue.

*Nancy Swell
and her lemon pie*

1 cup sugar   4 eggs, separated
5 Tbs. cornstarch   1½ cup water
2 large lemons, juice and zest (½ cup juice)
2 Tbs. butter   Pinch salt
9-inch blind-baked pie crust

Cook the sugar, cornstarch, and water until thickened and clear. In a separate bowl, beat the yolks and save the whites to make meringue. (See page 16.) Pour a little of the hot mixture into beaten egg yolks and whisk; then add the tempered yolks back into the pan and simmer 3 minutes. Remove from heat and stir in butter. Strain through a mesh sieve. Then stir in juice and rind. Pour hot filling into cooled, baked crust. Top with meringue and bake in a 350° oven for 15 minutes.

LEMON PIES

TWO CRUST LEMON PIE "RECEIPT" 1884
From a 19th-century Pennsylvania Handwritten Recipe Journal

Our good natured office staff has been taste-testing an awful lot of pies lately. So when our Marketing Director, David Currier, said to me days after sampling, "I just can't stop thinking about that lemon pie," I knew we had a winner. It's a beautiful and twangy old, old, old-timey pie that's a snap to make and a good choice for those of us who aren't wild about meringue.

WONDERFUL LEMON PIE! SUCH FLAKY TENDER CRUST

"To make a good Lemon Pie, take the juice and grated rind of one lemon, one cup of water, one tablespoonful of cornstarch, one cup of sugar, one egg, and a piece of butter the size of a small egg. Boil the water, wet the cornstarch with a little cold water and stir it in; when it boils up, pour it on the sugar and butter; after it cools, add the egg and lemon; bake with an under and upper crust. This makes the best Lemon Pie that it was ever my good fortune to taste."

Author's note: I really want you to try this pie, so here's an easier version. I've cut down on the sugar and water for increased "twang."

¾ **cup sugar**	**1 egg**
¾ **cup cold water**	**1 large lemon, juice and rind**
1 heaping Tbs. cornstarch	**1 Tbs. butter**

Stir cornstarch into the water, add sugar and simmer on low heat about three minutes. Let cool a few minutes while you roll out your crust. Whisk in whole egg, lemon juice and rind, and pour into an 8-inch unbaked crust. You can add a top crust if you like, but it's not necessary. Bake on bottom rack of oven at 375° for about 30 minutes until filling bubbles and crust is brown. Let it cool to room temperature, then refrigerate until firm. Serve with a little whipped cream.

Lemon Pie

Lemon Sponge Pie
Larkin Housewives Cookbook, 1915

Now this is a fun, easy, and tasty pie with a layer of cake covering a lemon cream filling. It's really a 19th century lemon sponge pudding baked in a pie shell. The Amish, known for their cake/pie combinations probably added the pie crust. Also known as Lemon Cake Pie, it was a popular dessert up through the 1950s.

¾ cup sugar	1 large lemon, juice and rind
2 eggs, separated	3 Tbs. flour
3 Tbs. butter, softened	1 cup milk

Beat sugar, egg yolks, and butter. Add lemon juice, rind (zest), and flour and mix together. Add milk, then fold in the egg whites, stiffly beaten. Bake three-fourths of an hour in a slow oven using only one crust.

Author's note: Start it off on lowest shelf of a preheated 400° oven for 10 minutes, then turn oven to 350° and bake for another 30 minutes, or until firm. Cover top with foil tent if getting dark too fast.

Izetta's Lemon Custard Pie
1910 Massachusetts Handwritten Cooking Journal

An earlier version of lemon cake/sponge pie by another name, though the recipe is nearly identical. Vintage handwritten cooking journals are story-books with pages reflecting the cooking abilities, tastes, interests and daily activities of their owners. Don't let them slip out of your family!

"Juice and grated rind of 1 lemon, 1 cup sugar, yolks of 2 eggs well beaten, 2 tablespoons flour, 1 cup sweet milk and small piece of butter. Mix in above order and last add whites of eggs beaten stiff. Stir in lightly till mixed. Bake with one crust."

CREAM PIES

C ream pies are an old-time American favorite. The custard filling is cooked separately, poured into a pre-baked crust, then topped with a mountain of meringue that's then baked a golden brown. Remember ... lemon, chocolate, coconut, and banana cream pies are "a masculine favorite." But plenty of women are crazy about them, too. They take some practice to get right, so my best advice is to eat at lots of diners that specialize in cream pies, and see if you can sweet-talk the cooks into sharing a few pointers with you.

Aunt Chick's Cream Pie Tips

To prevent runny filling:
> •*Add lemon juice and eggs after the filling has been thick*
> *ened with cornstarch or flour.*
> •*Continue to cook fillings after adding eggs at least 3*
> *minutes in order to "set" the eggs.*

To prevent soggy crust:
> *Be sure your filling is cooled to room temperature before*
> *adding to your cooled crust.*

To change recipe, reducing eggs from three to two:
> *Add an extra tablespoon of cornstarch or flour.*

CREAM PIES

Martha Whaley, born in the Sugarlands near Gatlinburg, Tennessee, in 1910 confesses, "I don't know how many pies I've made, maybe thousands." She and her 10 brothers and sisters were raised in a two-room handhewn log cabin in what is now the Smoky Mountains National Park.

As a child, Martha recalls picking the abundant fruit that grew wild in the mountains for cobblers, dumplings, and pies. "We picked wild blackberries, black and yellow raspberries, super sweet wild strawberries, and gooseberries. The woods were full of huckleberries (wild blueberries,) and my family tended an apple orchard of 150 trees. We raised varieties you never hear of now. There were Abraham, Sheepnose, Rusty Coat, Green Pippin, Sour John, Black Limbertwigs, Grimes Golden, Red June, and White June. My favorite pie apple is what we called Sour Early Harvest. Now, I just use Granny Smith apples in my pies."

"We canned berries and peaches, and dried the apples. My dad made a dry kiln with a furnace for the apples. We had a great hand-cranked peeler, and folks would come over for peelin' parties and we'd all get our apples dried for the winter."

Photo by Richard Renfro

At 94, Martha still makes three pies a week and gives them to her lucky friends. She says, "coconut cream is what most people like best, but I like fruit pie myself." My favorite pie is anything Martha makes, she has the magic touch that grew out of a lifetime of good living. I'm hoping that after making about a thousand more pies, mine will be half as good as hers!

Martha Whaley with her chocolate cream pie.

CREAM PIES

MARTHA'S VANILLA CREAM PIE

2 cups whole milk
5 Tbs. flour
½ cup sugar

3 eggs, separated
1 tsp. vanilla
1 Tbs. butter

Heat milk but don't boil. Sift flour and sugar together, then whisk into the hot milk. Cook in double boiler 15 minutes until thickened. Take about ½ cup of your milk mixture and whisk it into the egg yolks (or you'll get scrambled eggs.) Return that mixture back into the rest of the ingredients in your saucepan, and cook another 10 minutes on low heat until very thick. Remove from heat and stir in vanilla and butter. Pour into a baked pie shell, cover with Martha's meringue while still hot, being sure to bring the meringue all the way to the edges.

COCONUT CREAM

Add one cup shredded coconut to vanilla cream filling before pouring into pie shell. Sprinkle more on top of meringue before baking.

CHOCOLATE CREAM

Stir in 4 oz. melted bittersweet chocolate to vanilla cream filling at the end.

BANANA CREAM

Placed 2 or more sliced bananas (according to your taste) between 2 layers of the vanilla cream filling.

MARTHA'S MERINGUE

Martha makes her meringue using the typical ingredients of 2 Tbs. sugar and ⅛ tsp. cream of tartar to each egg white, only hers is like a meringue cookie sitting on top of the filling. It is incredibly beautiful and delicious, and not foamy or squishy. Here's what she says she does: "I beat the heck out of the egg whites with my Kitchen Aid, and then I beat them some more. Heat your oven to 300° and leave the pie in there for 30 minutes."

CREAM PIES

You should have seen the grin on my husband's face when he walked in the living room one day and saw me reading my new vintage book called, *"A Thousand Ways to Please Your Husband."* The promise of pie was some consolation as I showed him the subtitle: *"The Romance of Cookery and Housekeeping With Bettina's Best Recipes."* As it turns out, Bettina was a fictitious, perky early-20th-century housewife who lived to cook, bake,

organize, shop, tidy the house, and yes, please her new husband, Bob. She can teach you how to take grass stains out of your white dress while you whip up this dandy and economical Long's Peak Orange Pie in your spick and span little kitchen. There's a series of three "Bettina's Best" books, written from 1917 and revised into the 1930s, and really, they are quite entertaining. You'll love this pie.

LONG'S PEAK ORANGE PIE
A Thousand Ways to Please Your Husband, 1932 version

1 baked pie shell	2 tsp. grated orange rind
3 egg yolks	3 Tbs. lemon juice
1 cup sugar (I use ½ cup)	2 tsp. grated lemon rind
4 Tbs. flour	Pinch salt
1 Cup orange juice	2 Tbs. butter

"Beat the yolks then add the sugar and beat until creamy. Add the flour, fruit juice, rinds, and salt. Cook in a double boiler until thickened (about 20 minutes,) stirring frequently. Then add the butter. Pour into a baked pie shell and cover with the meringue."

Author's note: This is an orange version of lemon meringue pie, but notice it's thickened with flour (as are Martha's cream pies on page 39), instead of more modern corn starch. Flour-thickened pies are dense and creamy and never watery. Add the lemon and orange zest at the very end in case you need to strain out any bits of cooked egg. Or follow the method for Martha's cream pies on page 39.

CUSTARD PIES

Custard pies look so easy to make. But guess what? They are fussy. The problem is that pie crust needs to be baked at 400° or more in order to stay flaky and crisp under the filling. And custard needs to be baked at 350° or else the eggs will separate and both you and the pie will weep. Thank goodness for Spry's 1940s spokeswoman, good old Aunt Jenny. She's going to tell us how to "slip" a custard pie!

1. Bake the pie shell separately in a 450° oven for 12 minutes until lightly browned. Let cool.

2. Butter the same size pie pan and pour in the custard. Set pan in larger pan of hot water and bake at 350° 35-40 minutes until it's set.

3. Let custard cool to room temperature.

4. Loosen custard from sides of pan with knife. Shake gently. Slide it quickly into baked pie shell. Allow it to settle a few minutes before serving.

AUNT JENNY'S BEST COCONUT CUSTARD PIE
Aunt Jenny's 12 Pies Husbands Love Best, 1952

Beat slightly 4 eggs. Add 2/3 cup sugar, ½ tsp. salt, 2 cups milk, 1 tsp. vanilla, and mix. Add ¾ cup shredded toasted coconut and pour into a buttered 9-inch pie pan. Sprinkle top with ¼ tsp. nutmeg and place the pan in a larger pan of hot water. Bake in a 350° oven 35-40 minutes, until a knife inserted in the middle comes out almost, but not totally clean. Cool the custard at room temperature. It will stick if you refrigerate it. Now slip as above.

CUSTARD PIES

In her gem of a cookbook, *How Mama Could Cook*, Dorothy Malone recollects life growing up in the 1920s with her dramatic, feminist, beautiful, and loving Mama. As it turns out, Mama's flair for life is reflected in each and every wonderful recipe in the book. With a splash of cordial here and a dash of brandy there, I've learned from Mama how you can add pizzazz to any dish you prepare. Ms. Malone definitely inherited her Mama's sense of humor as she shares some of her adventures growing up in her bubbly and outspoken family. Here's one of my favorites.

"Since Mama felt that a crisis demanded a splendidly outfitted stomach as the first line of defense, she served good food dramatically and then looked the crisis right in the teeth." The crisis at hand for the occasion of the Rum Bittersweet Pie was this:

Mama was miffed at her husband because he had informed her last minute that his two teetotaling spinster sisters would be coming for the weekend, and wouldn't she please outdo herself with the meals ... on a shoestring budget. With the $25.00 she

won from a contest where she took a *"rousing stand on the affirmative side of the question, "Should Women Vote?"* she put on the dog. Her daughter, Dorothy, writes, *"She plotted a dinner so redolent of nefarious spirits that we were afraid the room would burst into blue flame when Father lit his after-dinner cigar."* After a meal of ham with champagne gravy, salad dressed with wine, rum kumquats, peach cordial soaked fruit, rum pie, and brandied coffee, the loosened-up ladies fairly glowed and said it was *"the finest dinner they had ever eaten!"*

Pie Insults
Frank C. Brown Collection of North Carolina Folklore,1964

- *She's as short as pie crust.*
- *He wouldn't work in a pie factory if you'd give him a tastin' job.*

CUSTARD PIES

MAMA'S RUM BITTERSWEET PIE
How Mama Could Cook, 1946

This is Mama's version of the traditional southern Black Bottom Pie, and it is a beauty. The potent flavor of rum really gives it a kick, but you might find that the whipped cream is overkill. If so, just sprinkle the grated chocolate on top of the pie filling and chill.

1 Tbs. gelatin	1 tsp. vanilla
¼ cup cold water	2 Tbs. dark rum
2 cups milk	¼ tsp. cream of tartar
½ cup sugar	2 Tbs. confectioner's sugar
1¼ Tbs. cornstarch	1 cup sweet, whipped cream
4 eggs, separated	½ square grated chocolate
1½ squares bittersweet chocolate (about 2 oz.)	

"Soak the gelatin in cold water and set aside. Scald the milk, add the sugar and cornstarch, and whisk in the 4 egg yolks. Cook over simmering water, stirring constantly, for 20 minutes or until the custard coats a silver spoon. Take from the heat, and take out a cup of the custard. Add to it the (chopped) bittersweet chocolate and vanilla, and beat until blended. When cool, pour as a base layer into a baked pie shell, and put in the icebox. While the remaining custard is still hot, add the gelatin and cool, but don't let it stiffen. Make a meringue of the 4 egg whites, the confectioner's sugar and cream of tartar, and fold it into the custard mixture. Add the rum. As soon as the chocolate layer has set, cover it with the rum mixture and chill. Spread with sweetened whipped cream and sprinkle the grated chocolate over the top. Serve chilled."

Author's note: Four egg whites makes a mountain of fluffy meringue. I find that using two works best. I recommend using an Italian (cooked) meringue. Simmer 6 Tbs. of sugar with 3 Tbs. water to the hardball stage. Beat two egg whites with ¼ tsp. cream of tartar until stiff peaks form, then slowly add the syrup while beating on high speed. Beat another couple minutes on medium speed, until the mixture cools. Fold into cooled rum/custard mixture.

CUSTARD PIES

KEY LIME PIE

If inventor Gail Borden's 1840s Terraqueous Machine (a prairie schooner with a sail designed to go on land and water) had been a hit, maybe there would be no Key Lime Pie today. As it turned out, his wagon sailboat couldn't stay afloat with a crew on board. So in 1856, he came up with a way to condense milk. The rest is history. The pie has had many transformations over the years from being baked in a traditional pie crust to a no-bake version poured into a graham cracker crust. I find an all-butter crust adds a nice balance to the sweetness of the innards. Some recipes call for a meringue topping, some whipped cream. To prevent foodborne illness, the current recommended method is to bake the pie about 15 minutes in a moderate oven until the filling reaches about 160°.

½ cup fresh key lime juice plus 2 tsp. lime zest
3 egg yolks
1 can (14 oz.) sweetened condensed milk
1 9-inch blind baked all butter crust

Separate the eggs. Whisk together the yolks and milk. Then slowly add the lime juice and zest. Pour into the prepared crust and bake in a preheated 350° for 15 minutes. Cool to room temperature and refrigerate for 4 hours before serving.

Author's note: If you want to win a pie contest, then fancy this pie up by lining the pre-baked crust with chocolate ganache (page 22), before adding the lime custard. Bake as directed and when cool, top with a layer of your homemade key lime curd, then fresh berries and piped whipped cream.

Key Lime & Raspberry Pie   *Photo by Wes Erbsen*

CUSTARD PIES

SWEET POTATO PIE
Pawley's Island, South Carolina Cookbook, 1955

Delicious and healthy, this pie improves with age. Make it the day before you want to serve it. Refrigerate and cover pie loosely or the crust will get soggy.

2 cups mashed sweet potatoes	**2 eggs**
3 Tbs. butter	**1 cup rich milk**
½ to ¾ cup brown sugar	**Pinch salt**
1 tsp. cinnamon, pinch nutmeg, ½ tsp. ginger	

Boil (I prefer to roast) potatoes whole, then skin and mash. Adjust sugar to your taste and the sweetness of the potatoes. Mix all the ingredients well. Line a pie plate with pastry and put in potato mixture. Bake on lowest oven shelf at 350° for 50-60 minutes until center is set and crust is brown.

SLICED SWEET POTATO PIE
George Washington Carver, 1937

Scholar, agricultural researcher, and inventor of at least 100 products made from sweet potatoes, George Washington Carver dishes out this interesting version of a traditional southern pie. Just in case you don't have a potato farmer's appetite, you can skip the bottom crust, and substitute whole milk for the cream.

"Line a deep baking dish with a rich sheet of pastry. Parboil the number of potatoes desired. When two thirds done, remove the skins, slice lengthwise, very thin, cover the dish to a depth of 2 inches, sprinkle with ground allspice and a dash of ginger, cloves, and nutmeg. To a pie sufficient for six people, scatter around the top in small pieces, a lump of butter the size of a hen's egg; add one teacupful of sugar and ½ teacupful of molasses. Add ½ pint cream, dust a little flour over the top sparingly. Put on upper crust, crimp edges and bake in a moderate oven until done. Serve hot."

CUSTARD PIES

OLD SOUTH CHOCOLATE CHESS PIE

Also called a "sugar pie", this simple rich dessert is what it is. Sort of a chocolate brownie topped custard with a little crunch of cornmeal. Underbake it a little if you like gooey brownies ... we call intentionally underbaked pastries "sad" here in the southern Appalachian mountains. We also like our chocolate pound cakes sad!

6 Tbs. unsalted butter	3 Tbs. milk
3 oz. bittersweet chocolate	1 tsp. vanilla
1 cup sugar	2 eggs, beaten
¼ tsp. salt	
1 Tbs. cornmeal	
1 Tbs. flour (or all cornmeal)	

Preheat oven to 400° Melt butter with chocolate and cool. Combine with remaining ingredients. Stir well, and pour into an unbaked 9-inch flaky butter crust. Bake on bottom third of a 400° oven for 10 minutes then turn heat to 350°. Bake another 20 minutes until the chocolate innards puff up but still wiggle a little.

Lemon chess pie: Add juice and zest of a lemon, omit chocolate
Os-Good: Omit chocolate and add ½ cup each pecans and raisins

TRANSPARENT PUDDING
The Great Western Cook Book, or Table Receipts, 1857

"Take half a pound of loaf-sugar, put it in a saucepan; break on it eight eggs, beat them well together; then add half a pound of butter, beat it again; add a nutmeg, sit on the fire; stir it till it thickens a little, but do not let it cook. Spread your pans with rich crust, pour it in, and bake in a moderate oven."

CUSTARD PIES

OLSON'S PINTO BEAN PIE

Here's an interesting and tasty version of "mock" pecan pie that my friend Marylyn Huff makes. If you ask her, is it "PEE-CAN" or "PUH-KAHN?", she'll tell you this: "In Georgia, where I come from, a pee can is something you stick under the bed at night!!!" Her husband, Olson, is mighty fond of pinto beans, so when they eat pie, this is the one she makes.

Photo by Richard Renfro

Marylyn Huff and her Pinto Bean Pie

½ cup cooked pinto beans
½ cup butter (or less)
½ cup chopped pecans
1 cup sugar
Pinch salt

½ can angel flake coconut
2 eggs
1 tsp. vanilla

If you use canned pinto beans, be sure they're unseasoned. Mash them well and add a little of the broth. Beat eggs and add with all other ingredients. Mix well and pour into a 9-inch unbaked pie shell. Bake 45 minutes at 325° on lowest oven rack until done. Unlike traditional custard pies, this one freezes well.

Author's note: You can substitute brown sugar for half of the white, and if you're watching your fat intake, decrease the butter to ¼ cup.

Dried Apple Pies
The Ladies Home Journal, September, 1886

I hate, abhor, detest, despise,
Abominate dried apple pies!
Tread on my toes and tell me lies,
But don't give me dried apple pies!

NUT PIES

Pies are wrapped and ready for auction at a 1940 pie supper

CLASSIC PECAN PIE, 1930S STYLE

The pecan pies that grace our Thanksgiving and Christmas tables today are a relatively modern creation. We have Karo corn syrup to thank for popularizing this type of pecan pie beginning in the 1930s. Earlier pie bakers made similar pies from molasses, sorghum syrup or light cane syrup, depending on what was available locally. Nuts rarely showed up in these "syrup" pies with the exception of walnuts or hickory nuts, which were more typically sweetened with brown sugar, honey or maple syrup.

3 eggs	1 tsp. vanilla
1 cup dark Karo	Pinch salt
1 cup sugar	1 cup pecans
2 Tbs. melted butter	9-inch unbaked pastry shell

Beat eggs slightly, then add syrup, sugar, butter, vanilla and salt. Stir in pecans, and pour into pastry shell. Bake on bottom shelf of a 350° oven for 50-60 minutes. Serve cool.

NUT PIES

BOURBON PECAN PIE

Here's a pecan pie without the gooey filling under the nuts. The brown sugar gives it a pretty, crunchy, homey glaze on top.

¾ cup light corn syrup
2 cups whole pecans, lightly toasted

½ cup brown sugar	2 Tbs. melted butter
2 eggs	2 Tbs. Bourbon or brandy
¼ tsp. salt	1 tsp. vanilla

Coarsely chop the pecans. Whisk together remaining ingredients, and stir in the chopped nuts. Pour into unbaked 9-inch crust. Bake at 425° for 10 minutes in bottom third of oven, then reduce heat to 350° and bake another 30 minutes until golden brown on top.

VARIATIONS:
Sorghum: Substitute sorghum syrup for corn syrup. The best!
Chocolate: Melt 3 oz. bittersweet chocolate with the butter
Honey: Use half honey and half corn syrup
Maple: Substitute maple syrup for corn syrup; use half the sugar.
Honey Walnut: Substitute walnuts for the pecans, honey for half of the corn syrup, and add ¼ cup heavy cream instead of the bourbon.

LOUISIANA SALTED PEANUT PIE
French Acadia Cook Book, 1955

Make this terrific pie the day before you want to eat it, and serve well chilled with a little semisweet chocolate drizzled on top.

¾ cup white corn syrup	2 Tbs. melted butter
½ cup brown sugar	1 tsp. vanilla
2 eggs	1¼ cup peanuts

Coarsely chop very lightly salted peanuts. Blend other ingredients, and stir in peanuts. Bake on lowest shelf of a 350° oven for 45 minutes or until crust is light brown and filling firms up.

NUT PIES

OAT & COCONUT MOCK PECAN PIE

Popular in the 1930s, a time for "making-do," this caramely Oatmeal/Coconut Pie is delicious and simple to make. We freeze it and serve the rich pie by the thin, cold, slice-ful.

2 eggs, beaten

¼ cup sugar

A good pinch salt

2 Tbs. melted butter

½ cup light corn syrup

¼ sorghum syrup (molasses)

A handful chopped dark chocolate

½ cup shredded unsweetened coconut

1 cup old fashioned oats, toasted 15 minutes in a 350° oven

Combine ingredients and pour into an unbaked, fluted pie shell. Bake at 400° for 10 minutes, then turn oven to 350° and bake for another 30 minutes or so, until pie is set and top is caramelized.

Courtesy of the Library of Congress

Thanksgiving pies, 1940   *Photo by Jack Delano*

Pennsylvania Dutch Pies

Pie making is not a lost art in the Pennsylvania Dutch communities of Southeastern Pennsylvania. In fact, if you live on a farm in this area of the country, you probably had pie for breakfast. When Mennonites from German speaking areas of Europe settled here seeking refuge from religious persecution in the 1720s, they brought with them a distinctive style of cooking and baking. While the German influence is still reflected in the food, farm families adapted recipes to make do with what they had on hand in this part of the country.

The Pennsylvania German are famous for all sorts of pies, from traditional fruit to custard, but most unique are their cake/pie combinations. They're quick to make and hearty enough to sustain you for a couple hours' worth of plowing.

Shoofly Pie

Crumbs:

¾ cup flour	3 Tbs. butter
⅓ cup brown sugar	¼ tsp. cinnamon
Pinch salt	¼ tsp. ginger

Bottom Layer:

½ tsp. baking soda	½ cup molasses
½ cup boiling water	Unbaked 9 inch pie shell

Blend crumb mixture well until crumbly. Combine boiling water, molasses, and soda. Pour into an unbaked pie shell. Sprinkle crumb mixture on top of liquid ingredients. Bake in a 400° oven 15 minutes, then turn heat down to 325° and bake 20-30 minutes longer until springy and browned.

To Destroy Flies
The Happy Home Magazine, 1858

To one pint of milk add a quarter of a pound of raw sugar, and two ounces of ground pepper; simmer them together eight or ten minutes, and place it about in shallow dishes. The flies attack it greedily and are soon suffocated.

PENNSYLVANIA DUTCH PIES

Here's a simple Vanilla Crumb Pie that's so good, one bite will make your knees buckle. Not unlike its creator, Dee Dee Meyer Artman, this traditional pie is straight forward, unpretentious, and says "home." Dee Dee is well known in eastern

Photo by Marti Otto

Pennsylvania's Lancaster County for her great cooking and hospitality served up in her Smoketown restaurant called "Dinner With Dee Dee." And does she ever have a story to tell.

When Dee Dee and her husband moved to Pennsylvania twenty years ago, they lived without electricity and modern amenities as they created their family of six children. They were, at the time, members of the Brethern, an Anabaptist group of Christian believers like the Amish and the Mennonites. Dee Dee sewed all her children's clothes, tended the garden, kids, home, canned hundreds of quarts of produce, and cooked on a wood cookstove. To earn a living, they invited over 2,500 tourists a year into their home for old-fashioned Amish style dinners prepared by Dee Dee. After a few years, the family moved into a more modern house, and Dee Dee eventually opened her own restaurant. That's where you can find her today.

With seemingly boundless energy, Dee Dee bakes (12 pies daily), cooks, and entertains her guests with tunes on the piano in a warm atmosphere with all the touches of home. You're going to love her version of this bubbly, fragrant pie!

Pennsylvania Dutch Pies

Dee Dee's Vanilla Crumb Pie

Filling:

Combine in a saucepan:

> ¾ cup each of white and brown sugar
> One very heaping Tbs. flour
> 1½ cups water

Slowly, bring to a boil, stirring continuously. Remove from heat and add 2 tsp. vanilla. Set aside while you make the crust and crumb topping.

Crumb topping:

1 cup all purpose flour	½ tsp. baking soda
¼ cup sugar	½ tsp. cream of tartar
4 Tbs. butter	

Pour syrup into a 10-inch unbaked crust. Spread crumbs evenly on top. Bake at 375° for 40-45 minutes.

Dee Dee's Oil Crust

> 1 cup pastry flour
> ½ tsp. salt
> ¼ cup vegetable oil
> 2 Tbs. cold water

Mix flour and salt, then stir in oil until evenly mixed. Add water and mix well. Put the dough into the center of a 10-inch pie pan. Pat and spread the dough until it just covers the rim of the pie plate.

Photos by Richard Renfro

Pennsylvania Dutch Pies

Funny Cake Pie

Shoofly's playful cousin, Funny Cake, is actually a cobbler in a pie crust. To tell you the honest truth, I have funny cake fever. Who knew that you can spread a one-egg cake batter in a pie pan, and no matter what sauce you put on top, it will sink to the bottom? I started off with chocolate, then went on to blue-  *berry, raspberry, lemon, and cherry. Make it in a pie crust if you're planning on walking eight miles after you plow your fields, otherwise you can break from tradition, and bake it in a 9-inch pie plate without the crust.*

Cake:

1 cup all purpose flour	¼ cup butter (unsalted)
1 tsp. baking powder	½ cup milk
½ tsp. salt	1 tsp. vanilla
½-¾ cup sugar	1 egg

Cream sugar and butter, add egg and beat until combined. Sift flour, baking powder, and salt, and add alternately with the milk. Add vanilla and beat about a minute. Pour into a buttered 10 inch or a deep dish 9 inch pie plate. Pour filling on top and bake at 350° for 40 minutes or until cake is springy and browned.

Fillings:

Fudge:

3 Tbs. butter	½ cup water
½ cup sugar	Splash vanilla
2 oz. unsweetened baking chocolate	

Melt butter and chocolate on low, add sugar and bring to a boil. Add water and boil a couple minutes. Pour (don't spread) evenly on top of cake batter and bake as above.

Pennsylvania Dutch Pies

Fresh berries:

2 cups berries	Splash water
½ cup sugar	3 Tbs. butter
2 Tbs. light corn syrup	

Crush 1 cup berries in a saucepan. Add sugar, butter, and corn syrup. Slowly bring to a boil, then continue boiling for 2-3 minutes more. Add a little bit of water to bring your liquid to about ½ cup. (This is not an exact science, it will turn out good no matter what you do.) Add remaining cup of berries, pour mixture over the cake batter, and bake as above.

Sour cherries:

Make as with fresh berries, above, substituting 2 cups pitted cherries. If using canned cherries, add all the fruit and only ½ cup of the juice to the sugar, corn syrup and butter, then boil as above.

Lemon:

3 Tbs. butter	¾ cup water
½ cup sugar	1 lemon, juice and zest
2 Tbs. cornstarch	

Combine cornstarch, water, and sugar. Simmer until clear and thick. Stir in butter, lemon juice, and zest and proceed as above.

QUICK PIES

FRESH FRUIT MIRACLE COBBLER

It's a miracle. A quick, delicious cobbler you can whip up in a jiffy with all those berries you picked today. Any fruit will do, but plump blackberries or black raspberries are the best.

4 Tbs. melted butter	**¾ to 1 cup sugar**
1 cup milk	**1 cup self rising flour**
3 cups fresh berries	**1 tsp. vanilla**

Melt butter in a deep dish glass pie plate. Stir dry ingredients together with milk and vanilla just until no lumps remain. Pour batter on the melted butter. Sprinkle 3 cups fresh berries on top and bake in a preheated 350° oven for about 35-40 minutes until lightly browned. I like to use less sugar in the recipe and sprinkle a little coarse sugar on top after it's baked about 15 minutes.

QUICK PIES

CRANBERRY SURPRISE PIE

This is what I call a "flip-pie." It's baked with the filling on the bottom, and as you take it from the oven, you flip it out onto a platter to serve. If you had walked into my Aunt Mary's Athens, W.Va. kitchen in the fall of 1955, you'd have seen her serving this pretty and delicious seasonal dish to her appreciative afternoon bridge party guests.

Toss, and place in a buttered 9 inch pie plate:

1 cup fresh cranberries, chopped
¼ cup brown sugar
¼ cup chopped walnuts (measure after chopping)

Combine:

1 beaten egg **6 Tbs. melted butter**
½ cup flour **½ cup white sugar**
½ tsp. almond extract
1 Tbs. orange marmalade (optional, but good)

Spread the above batter over the cranberry mixture all the way to the sides of the pan. Bake in a 350° oven about 25 minutes until top is a medium brown. Loosen the edges and flip the pie over onto a plate as soon as you take it from the oven. Serve warm with a little vanilla ice cream or whipped cream if you like.

Pie-Lore
Frank C. Brown Collection of North Carolina Folklore

If you get a piece of pie at the table, cut off the point, and save it till last; then make a wish, be quiet, eat the point of pie, drink some water, and the wish will come true.

Another very effective way of wishing is to leave the tip of a piece of pie to eat for the last thing. After eating it, do not speak, and back out of the dining room. The wish made while eating the tip will then come true.

QUICK PIES

APRICOT SKILLET PIE
Farm Life Magazine, November, 1927

Here's another "flip-pie" made in an iron skillet.

"Two cups of brown sugar and four tablespoons of butter. Melt in iron skillet and pour in two cups of (canned) apricots. Stir all together and let cook at the boiling point. On top of this mixture pour a one-egg cake or a sponge cake batter, making the batter a little stiffer than for ordinary cake. Bake in oven. When done turn out on platter and serve either cold or hot with whipped cream."
Author's note: ½ cup brown sugar is plenty. Drain the fruit first.

Photo by Marion Wolcott Post courtesy of the Library of Congress

*"Many parents and young people from the school and nearby communities attend the **pie supper**, given by the school to raise money for additional repairs and supplies. Each pie is auctioned off to the highest bidder, sometimes bringing a good deal, since the girl's "boyfriend" usually wins and has the privilege of eating it with her afterwards."*
Brethitt County, Kentucky, 1940

Quick Pies

Aunt Jenny's Honey Apple Dumplings
Good Cooking Made Easy With Spry, 1942

"Sweet and sugarless, an old favorite with a new twist." Sugarless as in no sugar because this is a World War II sugar shortage recipe. Aunt Jenny boasts, *"This mellow-rich honey sauce bakes into a beautiful glaze over the tender, golden dumpling crust. Honey not only sweetens the dumplings, but adds a delicious flavor to the tart apples."* Feel free to use unbaked pie crust squares instead of the biscuit dough.

2 cups flour	6 medium sized apples
1½ tsp. baking powder	1 Tbs. lemon juice
½ tsp. salt	3 Tbs. honey
½ cup Spry (use butter)	Pinch salt
½ cup milk (give or take)	

Sift flour, baking powder, and salt. Cut in Spry (butter) fine. Add milk gradually, mixing until a soft dough forms that you can roll out. Roll into rectangle 12 x 18 inches. Cut into 6 squares. Place a cored, peeled apple in each square. Fill centers with ingredients in right column. Moisten edges of dough to top of apple and press edges firmly together. Place in a 10 x 10 x 2 inch Sprycoated pan. Pour Honey Sauce over dumplings and bake in a hot 400° oven 30-35 minutes. Baste occasionally while baking.

Honey Sauce:
½ cup honey, 1 cup water, 2 Tbs. butter, 2 Tbs. Spry (omit), ¼ tsp. salt. Boil together for 5 minutes.

QUICK PIES

FRUIT CRISP

A fantastic and uncomplicated way to showcase your just harvested bounty of summer fruit. Serve in bowls topped with a scoop of fresh-churned creamy ice cream.

Topping for 6 cups of fruit:

5 Tbs. butter
¾ cup all purpose flour
4 Tbs. brown sugar
½ cup chopped nuts (walnuts or pecans)
Pinch salt

Rub butter into other ingredients until clumps form. Spread on top of fruit filling. You can add old-fashioned oats for extra crunch. Just decrease flour to ½ cup, and add ¾ cup oats. Bake at 375° in a clear glass casserole on lower rack of oven until filling bubbles and you can see from looking at the underside of the dish that no white cornstarch remains.

Apple: Peel and slice your apples, add a few tablespoons sugar and a sprinkle of cinnamon.
Peach: Remove skins by dipping in boiling water 30 seconds. Slice, sweeten, and stir in 2 Tbs. cornstarch or flour.
Berry: To 6 cups fruit, add ½-¾ cup sugar, depending on sweetness of your fruit and your taste. Stir in 3 Tbs. cornstarch or tapioca starch. If your fruit is dry, sprinkle with a little water or flavored liquor like Chambord so the cornstarch and sugar can coat the berries.

Here's how you make a rope crust. They make it look so easy!

Pinch upstanding rim between thumb and bent forefinger, making sharp crimps that hold their shape in baking.

HOLIDAY PIES

The winning bidder samples his pie with the baker at a pie auction in 1940.

MRS. PAINTER'S PUMPKIN PIE
The Art of Cooking in Salem, West Virginia, 1960

Here's a good old-fashioned creamy and firm pumpkin pie that is our family's favorite. While it's plenty good for Thanksgiving dessert, we fight over it for breakfast.

1½ cups pumpkin puree	¾ cup brown sugar
1 cup evaporated milk	Pinch salt
1 egg	1 Tbs. flour
1 tsp. each cinnamon and ginger	
Dash of freshly grated nutmeg	

Mix all ingredients well, and pour into an unbaked 9-inch pie shell. Bake in a 425° oven on the bottom rack for 10 minutes, then turn the oven to 350° and bake about 35 minutes or until the middle no longer wiggles.

HOLIDAY PIES

PUMPKIN PIE WITH A GINGERSNAP CRUST

No doubt about it, this is a chiffon pie. It comes from the era of the fluffy pie, straight out of my Aunt Mary's 1955, Wytheville, Va. St. Paul's Methodist Church Cookbook. Be aware that the pie contains uncooked egg whites.

1 envelope unflavored gelatin	1 tsp. ginger
½ cup cold water	1 tsp. cinnamon
1 can pumpkin (2 cups)	Pinch salt
1 cup brown sugar	3 eggs, separated
2 Tbs. white sugar	

Sprinkle gelatin over cold water to soften. Combine in saucepan: pumpkin, brown sugar, spices, and salt. Beat egg yolks slightly and add to pumpkin mixture. Cook over low heat, stirring constantly, until thickened. Add softened gelatin to hot mixture, stir until dissolved.

Chill until slightly thickened. Beat egg whites until stiff but not dry, beat in granulated sugar and fold into cooled pumpkin mixture. Pour into crumb crust. Serve chilled pie with whipped cream.

Gingersnap Crumb Crust:
1¼ cup gingersnap crumbs
5 Tbs. melted butter

Combine, and press into a 9-inch pie pan. Bake 5 minutes at 350° until lightly browned. Chill.

PUMPION PIE
The Cook Not Mad, 1831

"One quart of milk or cream, one pint of strained pumpion (pumpkin), six eggs, add ginger and sweeten to your taste. We have seen excellent pumpion pie made by nicely paring the pumpion before stewing, and straining it through a colender (sic) in lieu of a sieve."